One Day Crocheting Projects for Babies

Over 15 Crochet Projects for babies to Play, Wear & Snuggle

Table of Contents

Thank you for downloading this book, "One Day Crocheting Projects for Babies: Over 15 Crochet Projects for babies to Play, Wear, and Snuggle".

Please feel free to share this book with your friends and family. Please also take the time to write a short review on Amazon to share your thoughts.

An Introduction to Crocheting

There are a few basic crocheting techniques that you may need to get a hang of. So, here is a basic breakdown of them for you.

Slip Knot

1. Firstly, you need to make a loop and then hook another loop through the original loop.

2. Next you need to tighten the loop gently and carefully slide the knot up to the hook.

Chain Stitch

1. Do the whole 'yarn over hook' and then draw the yarn through to create a brand new loop without tightening the previous one.

2. Repeat the step above to form as many chains as the instructions suggest. It is important that you don't count the slip knot as a stitch.

Slip Stitch

1. Insert the hook into the work (it is the second chain from the hook), do a 'yarn over hook,' and draw the yarn through both the work and loop in one swift move.

2. In order to join a chain ring with a slip stitch, you must insert a hook into the first chain, then place the yarn over hook and next you should draw it through both the work and the yarn on hook in just a single move.

Single Crochet

1. Firstly, you need to insert the hook into the work (this is the second chain from the hook on the starting chain), *yarn over hook and draw yarn only through the work.

2. Place the yarn over the hook again and then carefully draw the yarn through both the loops.

3. Now one single crochet has been made. Insert the hook into the following stitch: now repeat from * in step one.

Half-Double Crochet

1. Firstly, place the yarn over the hook and insert it into the work (it is the third chain from the hook on the starting chain).

2. *Yarn over hook and draw through the work only.

3. Then place the yarn over the hook again and draw through all three loops.

4. Now that one-half double crochet made, you should place the yarn over the hook again and insert it into the next stitch, then repeat from step two.

Double Crochet

1. Place the yarn over the hook and insert the hook into the work (this is the fourth chain from the hook on the starting chain).

2. Place the yarn over hook and draw through the work only.

3. Then place the yarn over the hook and draw through the first two loops on the hook only.

4. Next, place the yarn over hook and draw through the last two loops.

5. Now one double crochet has been created. So to repeat this process; place the yarn over the hook then insert it into the following stitch and repeat from step two.

Triple Crochet

1. Yarn over hook twice, then insert hook into next stitch.

2. Yarn over hook and draw yarn through stitch - (there are four loop on the hook)

3. Loop yarn over hook and draw through two loops, (there are now three loops remaining on the hook).

4. Yarn over hook and draw through two loops.

5. Again, loop yarn over hook and draw through the last two loops on the hook (there is now one loop remaining.)

This completes one triple crochet.

Double Crochet Front Post

1. Work a round of normal double crochet for the first round and then turn.
2. Chain two for your first double crochet.
3. Yarn over and insert the crochet hook from the front to the back between the posts of the first and the second double crochet of the round underneath and then from the back to the front again between the posts of the second and the third stitches.
4. Yarn over and pull the yarn around the post of the stitch.
5. Yarn over and draw the yarn through the two loops on the hook, two times.

Double Crochet Front Post

1. Work a round of normal double crochet for the first round and then turn.
2. Chain two for your first double crochet.
3. Yarn over and insert the crochet hook from the back to the front between the posts of the first and the second double crochet of the round underneath and then from the front to the back again between the posts of the second and the third stitches.
4. Yarn over and pull the yarn around the post of the stitch.
5. Yarn over and draw the yarn through the two loops on the hook, two times.

Triple Crochet Front Post

1. Yarn over hook. Insert the hook horizontally from the right to the left in front of the post of the next stitch.

2. Pull up a loop (Yarn over hook and draw through two loops on the hook) two more times.

Triple Crochet Back Post

1. Yarn over hook. Insert the hook horizontally from the left to the right in front of the post of the next stitch.

2. Pull up a loop (Yarn over hook and draw through two loops on the hook) two more times.

Popcorn

1. Double crochet in the next stitch.

2. Remove the hook and insert in the first double crochet of the group, catch the loop of the last double crochet and pull through the first double crochet, making sure that the popcorn pattern is on the right side of the work.

Cluster

Yarn over, insert hook in indicated stitch and draw up a loop, yarn over and draw through two loops on hook; [yarn over, insert hook in same stitch and draw up a loop, yarn over and draw through two loops on hook] three times; yarn over and draw through all five loops on hook.

Now that you have a basic understanding of both the crocheting and the knitting techniques, we can get started!

BABY AFGHAN BLANKET

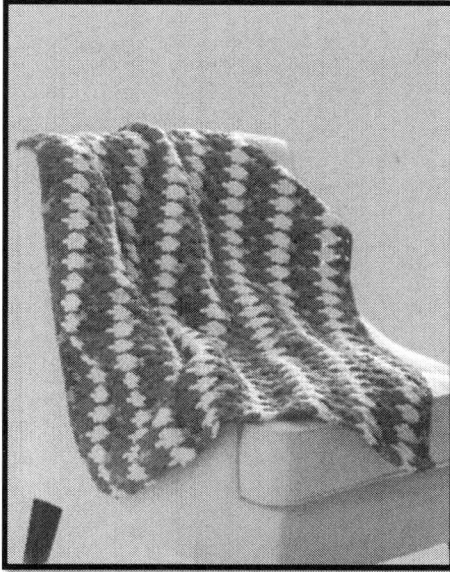

MATERIALS

- Three Different Colors of Yarn – Four Balls Each
- Size U.S. I/9 (Five Point Five Millimeters) Crochet Hook

MEASUREMENTS

- Approximately Forty Eight Inches x Sixty Inches [One Hundred and Twenty Two x One Hundred and Fifty Two Point Five Centimeters].

GAUGE

- Twelve Double Crochet and Six and a Half Rounds = Four Inches [Ten Centimeters].

INSTRUCTIONS

Notes:

When joining the different colors together, work to the last two loops on the hook of the first color. Draw the new color through the last two loops and proceed. Chain three at the beginning of round is regarded as a double crochet throughout the process.

Stripe Pat

Using the Main Color, work two rounds. Using Color A, work two rounds. Using Color B, work two rounds. These six rounds form a Striped Pattern. Using the Main Color, chain one hundred and forty five. Mark every twenty fifth chain for easier counting.

First Round: One double crochet in the fourth chain from hook (Counts as two double crochet). One double crochet in the next chain. * Chain one. Miss the next chain. One double crochet in each of the next three chains. Repeat from * to the end of the chain. Turn.

Second Round: Chain three. One double crochet in each of the next two double crochet. * Chain one. Miss the next chain. One double crochet in each of the next three double crochet. Repeat from * to the end of the round. Join Color A. Turn.

Third Round: Using Color A, chain four (counts as double crochet and chain one). Miss the next double crochet. One double crochet in the next double crochet. * Yarn over hook and draw up a long loop in one space chain two rounds below. (Yarn over hook and pull through two loops on the hook) two times – extended double crochet is made. One double crochet in the next double crochet. Chain one. Miss the next double crochet. Repeat from * to the end of the round. Turn.

Fourth Round: Chain four (counts as double crochet and chain one). Miss the next chain. * One double crochet in each of the next three stitches. Chain one. Miss the next chain. Repeat from * ending with one double crochet in the third chain of turning chain. Join Color B. Turn.

Fifth Round: Using Color B, chain three. One extended double crochet. One double crochet in the next double crochet. * Chain one. Miss the next double crochet. One double crochet in the next double crochet. One extended double crochet. One double crochet in the next double crochet. Repeat from * to the end of the round. Turn.

Sixth Round: Chain three. One double crochet in each of the next two stitches. * Chain one. Miss the next chain. One double crochet in each of the next three stitches. Repeat from * to the end of the round. Join COLOR A. Turn. First six rounds of Striped Pattern are complete. Keep continuing the Stripe Pattern, repeat the third to sixth rounds until the work from the beginning measures approximately sixty inches [one hundred and fifty two point five centimeters], ending with two rounds of Color A. Fasten off.

BABY SNOW WHITE POM POM HAT

MEASUREMENTS:

To fit baby's head 3/6 (6/12-18/24) mos.

MATERIALS:

- White Yarn (One - Two Balls)
- Crochet Hook (8 mm)
- Thread and Needle
- Scissors

INSTRUCTIONS:

These instructions are written for the smallest size. If there are changes that need to be made for the larger sizes, the instructions will be written in the ( ).

Chain 47 (56-61).

First Round: One single crochet in the second chain from the hook.

Now complete one single crochet in each chain to the end of the chain. Turn. 46 (55-60) single crochet.

Second Round: Chain one. Then complete one single crochet in each single crochet to the end of the round. Turn.

Third Round: Chain one. (One single crochet. Two double crochet) in the first single crochet. * Skip the next two single crochet. (One single crochet. Two double crochet) in the next single crochet). Repeat form * to the last three single crochet. Skip the next two single crochet. Then complete one single crochet in the last single crochet. Turn.

Fourth Round: Chain one. (One single crochet. Two double crochet) in the first single crochet. * Skip the next two double crochet. (One single crochet. Two double crochet) in the next double crochet. Now, repeat from * to the last single crochet in the last single crochet. Turn.

Repeat the last round for the pattern until the work from the beginning measures 6 (7-8)" [15 (18-20.5) cm]. Fasten off. Fold the piece in half. Using a thread and needle, sew the side and the top seam together.

Pompom (make 2)

Twirl the yarn around three of your fingers approximately fifty times. Then remove the yarn from your fingers and tie them tightly in the center. Cut through each side of the loops. Trim to a smooth, round shape. Using the thread and needle, sew one pompom to each top corner of the hat.

BABY CLUCK CLUCK MINI BAG

MATERIALS

- Two Different Colors of Yarn – One Ball of Each, Dark Brown and Light Brown
- Small Quantities of Red and Orange Yarn
- Size U.S. F/5 (3.75 mm) Crochet Hook
- Two Stitch Markers
- Six Inch (Fifteen Centimeters) Zipper
- Two Glue On Googly Eyes
- Glue

MEASUREMENTS

- Approximately Five Inches [Twelve Point Five Centimeters] Wide x Four and a Quarter Inches [Eleven Centimeters] High.

GAUGE

- Sixteen Single Crochet and Seventeenth Rounds = Four Inches [Ten Centimeters].

INSTRUCTIONS

Body

Using the Main Color, chain six.

First Round: One single crochet in the second chain from the hook. One single crochet in each of the next three single crochet. Three single crochet in the last single crochet. Working into the opposite side of the chain, one single crochet in each of the next three single crochet. Two single crochet in the last single crochet. Join with the slip stitch to the first single crochet. Twelve single crochet.

Second Round: Chain one. One single crochet in each of the first five single crochet. Three single crochet in the next single crochet. One single crochet in each of the next five single crochet. Three single crochet in the last single crochet. Join with a slip stitch to the first single crochet sixteen single crochet.

Third Round: Chain one. One single crochet in each of the first six single crochet. Five single crochet in the next single crochet. One single crochet in each of the next seven single crochet. Five single crochet in the next single crochet. One single crochet in the last single crochet. Join with the slip stitch to the first single crochet. Twenty-four single crochet.

Fourth Round: Chain one. One single crochet in each of the first seven single crochet. Two single crochet in the next single crochet. Three single crochet in the next single crochet. Two single crochet in the next single crochet. One single crochet in each of the next nine single crochet. Two single crochet in the next single crochet. One single crochet in each of the last two single crochet. Join with a slip stitch to the first single crochet. Thirty-two single crochet.

Fifth and Sixth Rounds: Chain one. One single crochet in each single crochet around. Join with a slip stich to the first single crochet.

Seventh Round: Chain one. One single crochet in each of the first ten single crochet. Three single crochet in the next single crochet One single crochet in each of the next fifteen single crochet. Three single crochet in the next single crochet. One single crochet in each of the next fifteen single crochet. Three single crochet in the next single crochet. One single crochet in each of the next fifteen single crochet. Three single crochet in the next single crochet. One single crochet in each of the last five single crochet. Join with a slip stitch to the first single crochet. Thirty-six single crochet.

Eighth Round: Chain one. One single crochet in each of the first eleven single crochet. Three single crochet in the next single crochet, placing marker on the center single crochet. One single crochet in each of the next seventeen single crochet. Three single crochet in the next single crochet. One single crochet in each of the next six single crochet. Join with a slip stitch to the first single crochet. Forty single crochet.

Ninth to Thirteenth Rounds: Chain one. One single crochet in each single crochet around. Join with a slip stitch to the first single crochet.

Shape Head and Tails – Fourteenth Round: Skip the first single crochet (where the last slip stitch was worked). Slip stitch in each of the next five single crochet. One single crochet in each of the next thirteen single crochet. Slip stitch in each of the next six single crochet. One single crochet in each of the next fifteen single crochet. Join with a slip stitch to the first slip stitch.

Fifteenth Round: Skip the first single crochet (where last slip stitch was worked). Slip stitch in each of the next six stitches. One single crochet in each of the next eleven single crochet. Slip stitch in each of next seven stitches. One single crochet in each of the next fifteen single crochet. Join with a slip stitch to the first slip stitch.

Sixteenth Round: Skip the first single crochet (where last slip stitch was worked). Slip stitch in each of the next seven stitch. One single crochet in each of the next nine stitches. One single crochet in the next single crochet. One half double crochet in each of the next eleven single crochet. One single crochet in the next single crochet. Slip stitch in the last single crochet. Join with a slip stitch to the first slip stitch.

Seventeenth Round: Skip the first single crochet (where the last slip stitch was worked). Slip stitch in each of the next eight stitches. One single crochet in each of the next seven single crochet, placing a maker on the center single crochet (tail end). Slip stitch in each of the next eleven stitches. One single crochet in the next single crochet. One half double crochet in each of the next nine half double crochet, placing a marker on the center half double crochet (head end). One single crochet in the last single crochet. Slip stitch in each of the last two stitches. Join with a slip stitch to the first slip stitch. Fasten off.

Wing (Make Two)

Using Color A, chain six.

First Round: One single crochet in the second chain from the hook. One single crochet in each of the next three single crochet. Three single crochet in the last single crochet. Working into the opposite side of the chain, one single crochet in each of the next three single crochet. Two single crochet in the last single crochet. Join with a slip stitch to the first single crochet. Twelve single crochet.

Second Round: Chain one. One single crochet in each of the first five single crochet. Three single crochet in the next single crochet. One single crochet in each of the next five single crochet. Three single crochet in the last single crochet. Join with a slip stitch to the first single crochet sixteen single crochet.

Third Round: Chain one. One single crochet in each of the first six single crochet. Three single crochet in the next single crochet. One single crochet in each of the next seven single crochet. Chain four. (One triple. One double crochet. One half double crochet) in the next single crochet. One single crochet in the last single crochet. Join with a slip stitch to the first single crochet. Fasten off.

Tail Feather

 Using Color A, chain seven.

First Round: One double triple. (Chain six. Slip stitch. Chain six. One double triple) twice. Chain six. Slip stitch] all in the seventh chain from the hook. Fasten off.

Comb

Using some red yarn, chain four.

First Round: Wrong Side. One single crochet in the second chain from the hook. Three single crochet in the next chain. One single crochet in the last chain. Turn. Four single crochet.

Second Round: Chain four. Skip the first single crochet. One single crochet in the next single crochet. (Chain four. One single crochet in the next single crochet) three times. Fasten off.

Beak

Using orange yarn, chain three.

First Round: One single crochet in the second chain from the hook. One half double crochet in the last chain. Fasten off.

FINISHING

Work running stitch embroidery using the Main Color around the third round of the Wing. Using a thread and needle, attach one Wing to each side of the Body. At the markers, fold the Body in half. Then attach the top of the Head using the needle and thread along the final round for one inch [two point five centimeters]. Continue by sewing the zipper in position along the top edge (after the seam of the head). Sew the Tail Feather and Comb in position and then attach the Beak's side edge in position to create a triangular shape. Finally, using the glue, attach the googly eyes in position.

BABY EASY GOING CROCHET BLANKET

MATERIALS

- One Color of Yarn – Twelve Balls
- Size U.S. S (Nineteen Millimeters) Crochet Hook

MEASUREMENTS

- Approximately Forty-Eight Inches x Fifty-Six Inches [One Hundred and Twenty Two x One Hundred and Forty Two Centimeters].

GAUGE

- Four Single Crochet and Four Rounds = Four Inches [Ten Centimeters].

INSTRUCTIONS

Note:

The blanket is reversible. There is no right side or wrong side. Chain fifty-eight.

First Round: One single crochet in the second chain from the hook. * Chain one. Skip the next chain. One single crochet in the next chain. Repeat from * to the end of the chain. Turn. Fifty- seven stitches.

Second Round; Chain three (counts as a half double crochet and chain one). * Half double crochet two stitches together over the next one space chain and the next single crochet. Chain one. Repeat from * to the end of the round. Turn.

Third Round: Chain one. One single crochet in the first half double crochet the next two stitches together. One single crochet in the next one space chain. * Chain one. Skip the net half double crochet the next two stitches together. One single crochet in the next one space chain. Repeat from * across, ending with one single crochet in the second chain of turning chain.

Fourth Round: Chain two (counts as a half double crochet). Half double crochet the next two stitches together over the first two single crochet. Chain one. * Half double crochet the next two stitches together over the next one space chain and the next single crochet. Chain one. Repeat from * to the last three stitches. Half double crochet the next two stitches together over the next one space chain and the next single crochet. One half double crochet in the last single crochet. Turn.

Fifth Round: Chain one. One single crochet in the first half double crochet. * Chain one. Skip the next 'half double crochet the next two stitches together'. One single crochet in the next one space chain. Repeat from * to the last two stitches. Chain one. Skip the last 'half double crochet the next two stitches together'. One single crochet in the top of the turning chain. Turn. Repeat from the second to the fifth rounds to form a pattern until the work from the beginning measures approximately fifty-six inches [one hundred and forty two centimeters], ending on a third or fifth round of pattern. Do not fasten off.

Edging Round: Chain one. Work one round of single crochet evenly around the outer edges of the blanket. Join with a slip stitch to the first single crochet. Fasten off.

BABY BOLSTER

MATERIALS

- One Color of Yarn – Two Balls
- Size U.S. S (Nineteen Millimeters) Crochet Hook

MEASUREMENTS

- Bolster Pillow Forms Six Inches [Fifteen Centimeters] In Diameter x Fourteen Inches [Thirty Five Point Five Centimeters] Long.

GAUGE

- Four Half Double Crochet and Two and a Half Rounds = Four Inches [Ten Centimeters].

INSTRUCTIONS

Note:

Chain two at the beginning of rounds. Does not count as a stitch. Chain three.

First Round: Nine half double crochet in the third chain from the hook. Join with a slip stitch to the first half double crochet.

Second Round: Chain two. Two half double crochet in each of the half double crochet around. Join with a slip stitch to the first half double crochet. Eighteen half double crochet.

Third Round: Chain two. Working in the back loops only, one half double crochet in each half double crochet around. Join with a slip stitch to the first half double crochet.

Fourth Round: Chain two. * Working in horizontal bars created at the back of the work between the stitches of the previous round. One half double crochet in each half double crochet around. Do not join. Working in a spiral, repeat from * until the work from the third round measures approximately fourteen inches [thirty-five point five centimeters]. Insert pillow form.

Next Round: Chain two. Working in the back loops only, one half double crochet in each half double crochet around. Join with a slip stitch to the first half double crochet. Eighteen half double crochet.

Next Round: Chain two. * Half double crochet two stitches together. Repeat from * around. Join with a slip stitch to the first half double crochet. Nine stitches. Fasten off. Thread the ends through the remaining stitches and fasten them tightly.

Baby Cute Beanie

MATERIALS:

- One Color of Yarn (One Ball)
- Crochet Hook (3.75 mm)

INSTRUCTIONS:

These instructions are written for smallest size.

Note: Chain three at the beginning of the round counts as double crochet.

Chain four.

First Round: Eleven double crochet in the fourth chain from the hook. Join with a slip stitch to the top of chain three. Twelve double crochet.

Second Round: Chain three. One double crochet in the same space as the last slip stitch. * two double crochet in the next double crochet. Now, repeat from * around. Join with a slip stitch to the top of chain three. Twenty four double crochet.

Third Round: Chain three. * Two double crochet in the next double crochet. Now you should do one double crochet in the next double crochet. Then now repeat from * to the last double crochet. Two double crochet in the last double crochet. Join with a slip stitch to the top of chain three. Thirty six double crochet.

Fourth Round: Chain three. * Two double crochet in the next double crochet. Add one double crochet in each of the next two double crochet. Repeat from * to the last two double crochet. Two double crochet in the next double crochet. Now, add another one double crochet in the last double crochet. Join with a slip stitch to the top of chain three. Forty-eight double crochet.

Fifth Round: Chain three. * Two double crochet in the next double crochet. Now, you should do one double crochet in each of the next eleven (three - two) double crochet. Repeat from * to the last eleven (three - two) double crochet. Two double crochet in the next double crochet. Now add another double crochet in each of the last ten (two-one) double crochet. Join with a slip stitch to the top of chain three. Fifty-two (sixty – sixty four) double crochet.

Sixth Round: Chain three. Now you should do one double crochet in each double crochet around. Join with a slip stitch to the top of chain three. Repeat the last round until the work from the beginning measures 31/2 (41/2-41/2) inches.

Size Eighteen Months Only

First Round: Chain three. * One double crochet in each of the next fourteen double crochet. (Yarn over hook and draw up a loop in the next double crochet. Yarn over hook and draw through two loops on hook) twice. Yarn over hook and draw through all loops on the hook – double crochet two stitches together made. Now, repeat from * three more times. Join with a slip stitch to the top of chain three. Sixty double crochet.

All Sizes

Edging

First Round: Chain one. One single crochet in the same space as the last slip stitch. * Chain five. Miss the next three double crochets. Do one single crochet in the next double crochet. Repeat from * around, omitting single crochet at the end of the last repeat. Join with a slip stitch to the first single crochet.

Second Round: Chain five. * One single crochet in the next five-space chain. Chain two. (Yarn over hook and draw up a loop. Yarn over hook and draw through two loops on the hook) three times in the next single crochet. Yarn over hook and draw through all loops on the hook – creating a cluster. Chain two. One single crochet in the next five space chain. Chain five. Repeat from * across, ending with chain two. Slip stitch in the third chain of chain five.

Third Round: Chain one. One single crochet in the same space as the last slip stitch. * Chain five. Now add one single crochet in the next cluster. Chain five. One single crochet in the next five space chain. Repeat from * around, ending with chain five. Join with a slip stitch to the first single crochet. Fasten off.

BABY BOBBLE CROCHET AFGHAN

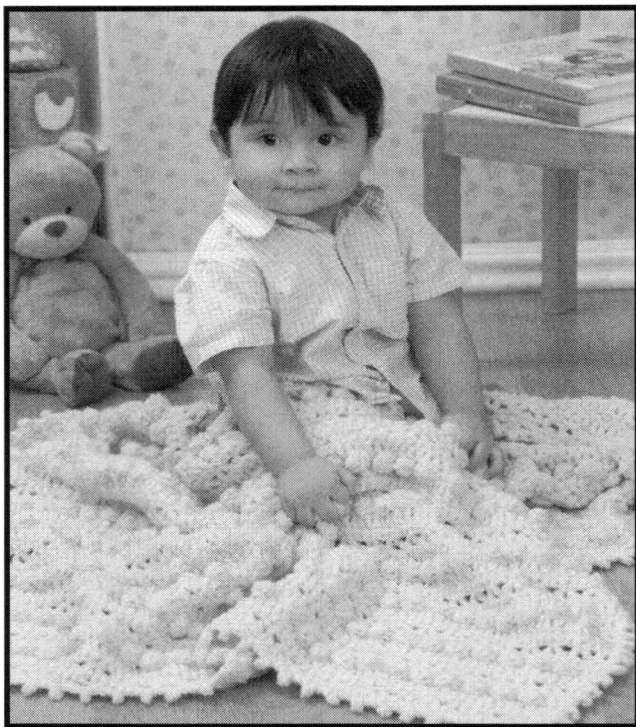

MEASUREMENTS:

Approximately 34 x 48 inches [86.5 x 122 centimeters]

MATERIALS:

- One Color of Yarn (6 Balls)
- Size 5 mm (U.S. H or 8) crochet hook

STITCH GLOSSARY Bobble = Working in front of the work, work five triple stitches in the one space chain two rows below until the one loop of each triple stitch remaining on the crochet hook. Yarn over hook and draw through all six loops on the hook.

INSTRUCTIONS:

Chain one hundred and twenty six.

First Round (Right Side): One single crochet in the second chain from the hook. One single crochet in the next chain. Chain one. Miss the next chain * One single crochet in each of the next eleven chains. Chain one. Miss the next chain. Repeat from * to the last two chains. One single crochet in each of the last two chain. Chain three. Turn.

Second Round: Miss the first single crochet. One double crochet in the next single crochet. Chain one. Miss the next one space chain. * One double crochet in each of the next eleven single crochet. Chain one. Miss the next one space chain. Repeat from * to the last two single crochet. One double crochet in each of the last two single crochet. Chain one. Turn.

Third Round: Chain one. One single crochet in each of the first two double crochet. Bobble = Working in front of the work, work five triple stitches in the one space chain two rows below until the one loop of each triple stitch remaining on the crochet hook. Yarn over hook and draw through all six loops on the hook in. * One single crochet in the next double crochet. Chain one. Miss the next double crochet. One single crochet in each of the next seven double crochet. Chain one. Miss the next double crochet. One single crochet tin the next double crochet. Bobble = Working in front of the work, work five triple stitches in the one space chain two rows below until the one loop of each triple stitch remaining on the crochet hook. Yarn over hook and draw through all six loops on the hook. Repeat form * to the last two double crochet. One single crochet in the next double crochet. One single crochet in the top of the turning chain. Chain three. Turn.

Fourth Round: Miss the first single crochet. One double crochet in each of the next three stitches. *Chain one. Miss the next one space chain. One double crochet in each of the next seven stitches. Chain one. Miss the next one space chain. One double crochet in each of the next three stitches. Repeat from * to the last stitch. One double crochet in the last single crochet. Chain one. Turn.

Fifth Round: One single crochet in each of the first four double crochet. * Bobble = Working in front of the work, work five triple stitches in the one space chain two rows below until the one loop of each triple stitch remaining on the crochet hook. Yarn over hook and draw through all six loops on the hook. One single crochet in the next double crochet. Chain one. Miss the next double crochet. One single crochet in each of the next three double crochet. Chain one. Miss the next double crochet. One single crochet in the next double crochet. Bobble = Working in front of the work, work five triple stitches in the one space chain two rows below until the one loop of each triple stitch remaining on the crochet hook. Yarn over hook and draw through all six loops on the hook. One single crochet in each of the next three double crochet. Repeat from * to the last stitch. One single crochet in the top of the turning chain. Chain three. Turn.

Sixth Round: Miss the first single crochet. One double crochet in each of the next five stitches. * Chain one. Miss the next one space chain. One double crochet in each of the next three stitches. Chain one. Miss the next one space chain. One double crochet in each of the next seven stitches. Repeat from * to the last ten stitches. Chain one. Miss the next one space chain. One double crochet in each of the next three stitches. Chain one. Miss the next one space chain. One double crochet in each of the next six stitches. Chain one. Turn.

Seventh Round: One single crochet in each of the first six double crochet. * Bobble = Working in front of the work, work five triple stitches in the one space chain two rows below until the one loop of each triple stitch remaining on the crochet hook. Yarn over hook and draw through all six loops on the hook. One single crochet in the next double crochet. Chain one. Miss the next double crochet. One single crochet in the next double crochet. Bobble = Working in front of the work, work five triple stitches in the one space chain two rows below until the one loop of each triple stitch remaining on the crochet hook. Yarn over hook and draw through all six loops on the hook. One single crochet in the next double crochet. Chain one. Miss the next double crochet. One single crochet in the next double crochet. Bobble = Working in front of the work, work five triple stitches in the one space chain two rows below until the one loop of each triple stitch remaining on the crochet hook. Yarn over hook and draw through all six loops on the hook. One single crochet in each of the next five double crochet. One single crochet in the top of the turning chain. Chain three. Turn.

Eighth Round: Miss the first single crochet. One double crochet in each of the next seven stitches. Chain one. Miss the next one space chain. *One double crochet in each of the next eleven stitches. Chain one. Miss the next one space chain. Repeat from * to the last eight stitches. One double crochet in each of the next eight stitches. Chain one. Turn.

Ninth Round: One single crochet in each of the first six double crochet. * Chain one. Miss the next double crochet. One single crochet in the next double crochet. Bobble = Working in front of the work, work five triple stitches in the one space chain two rows below until the one loop of each triple stitch remaining on the crochet hook. Yarn over hook and draw through all six loops on the hook. One single crochet in the next double crochet. Chain one. Miss the next double crochet. One single crochet in each of the next seven double crochet. Repeat from * to the last eleven stitches. Chain one. Miss the next double crochet. One single crochet in each of the next double crochet. Bobble = Working in front of the work, work five triple stitches in the one space chain two rows below until the one loop of each triple stitch remaining on the crochet hook. Yarn over hook and draw through all six loops on the hook. One single crochet in the next double crochet. Chain one. Miss the next double crochet. One single crochet in each of the next six double crochet. Chain three. Turn.

Tenth Round: Miss the first single crochet. One double crochet in each of the next five stitches. * Chain one. Miss the next one space chain. One double crochet in each of the next three stitches. Chain one. Miss the next one space chain. One double crochet in each of the next seven stitches. Repeat from * to the last ten stitches. Chain one. Miss the next one space chain. One double crochet in each of the next three stitches. Chain one. Miss the next one space chain. One double crochet in each of the next six stitches. Chain one. Turn.

Eleventh Round: One single crochet in each of the first four double crochet. *Chain one. Miss the next double crochet. One single crochet in the next double crochet. Bobble = Working in front of the work, work five triple stitches in the one space chain two rows below until the one loop of each triple stitch remaining on the crochet hook. Yarn over hook and draw through all six loops on the hook. One single crochet in each of the next three double crochet. Bobble = Working in front of the work, work five triple stitches in the one space chain two rows below until the one loop of each triple stitch remaining on the crochet hook. Yarn over hook and draw through all six loops on the hook. One single crochet in the next double crochet. Chain one. Miss the next double crochet. One single crochet in each of the next three double crochet. Repeat from * to the last stitch. One single crochet in the top of the turning chain. Chain three. Turn.

Twelfth Round: Miss the first single crochet. One double crochet in each of the next five stitches. * Chain one. Miss the next one space chain. One double crochet in each of the next three stitches. Chain one. Miss the next one space chain. One double crochet in each of the next seven stitches. Repeat from * to the last ten stitches. Chain one. Miss the next one space chain. One double crochet in each of the next three stitches. Chain one. Miss the next one space chain. One double crochet in each of the next six stitches. Chain one. Turn.

Thirteenth Round: One single crochet in each of the first two double crochet. Chain one. Miss the next double crochet. One single crochet in the next double crochet. *Bobble = Working in front of the work, work five triple stitches in the one space chain two rows below until the one loop of each triple stitch remaining on the crochet hook. Yarn over hook and draw through all six loops on the hook. One single crochet in each of the next seven double crochet. Bobble = Working in front of the work, work five triple stitches in the one space chain two rows below until the one loop of each triple stitch remaining on the crochet hook. Yarn over hook and draw through all six loops on the hook. One single crochet in the next double crochet. Chain one. Miss the next double crochet. One single crochet in the next double crochet. Repeat from * to the last stitch. One single crochet in the top of the turning chain. Chain three. Turn. Repeat the rounds between two and thirteen for the formation of the pattern.

Continue in pattern until the work from the beginning measures approximately 45 inches [114.5 centimeters], ending with a row three of pattern, and omitting the turning chain at the end of the last row. Fasten off.

Edging: Join the yarn with a slip stitch at the top right hand corner of the Afghan. Chain three. Work one round double crochet around the entire Afghan working three double crochet in the corners. Join with a slip stitch to the top of chain three. Work two more rounds of the double crochet like before. Fasten off.

BABY SOFT BLANKET

MATERIALS

1) One Color of Yarn – Two Balls
2) Size Four Millimeters (U.S. G or 6) Crochet Hook

MEASUREMENTS

Approximately Thirty-Six Inches [Ninety-One Point Five Centimeters] Wide x Thirty-Eight Inches [Ninety-Six Point Five] Long.

GAUGE

Nineteen Double Crochet and Ten Rounds = Four Inches [Ten Centimeters].

INSTRUCTIONS

Note:

Chain three and the beginning of round counts as double crochet.

Chain one hundred and sixty two.

Foundation Round: Right Side. One double crochet in the third chain from the hook (counts as two double crochet). * Chain one. Miss the next two chains. Three double crochet in the next chain. Repeat from * to the last three chains. Chain one. Miss the next two chains. Two double crochet in the last chain. Turn. Fifty-two three-double crochet groups.

First Round: Chain three. Miss the first two double crochet * (one double crochet. Chain one. One double crochet in the next one space chain – V Stitch made. Repeat from * to the last two double crochet. Miss the next double crochet. One double crochet in the top of the turning chain. Turn. Fifty-three V Stitches.

Second Round: Chain three. * Three double crochet in a one-space chain of the next V Stitch. Chain one. Repeat from * to the last V Stitch. Three double crochet in the last V Stitch. One double crochet in the top of the turning chain. Turn.

Third Round: Chain three. One double crochet in the first double crochet. * One V Stitch in the next one space chain. Repeat from * to the last double crochet. Two double crochet in the top of turning chain. Turn.

Fourth Round: Chain three. One double crochet in the next double crochet. Chain one. * Three double crochet in one space chain of the next V Stitch. Chain one. Repeat from * to the last two double crochet. One double crochet in the next double crochet. One double crochet in the top of the turning chain. Turn. Repeat the last four rounds until the work from the beginning measures thirty-five inches [eighty-nine centimeters], ending with a fourth round of pattern. Do not fasten off.

Edging

First Round: Chain one. Work one round of single crochet evenly around the Blanket, having three single crochet in the corners. Join with a slip stitch to the first single crochet.

Second Round: Chain one. One single crochet in the first single crochet. * Chain three. Slip stitch in the top of the single crochet – picot is made. One single crochet in each of the next two single crochet. Repeat from * around. Join with a slip stitch to the first single crochet. Fasten off.

BABY GRANNY SACK

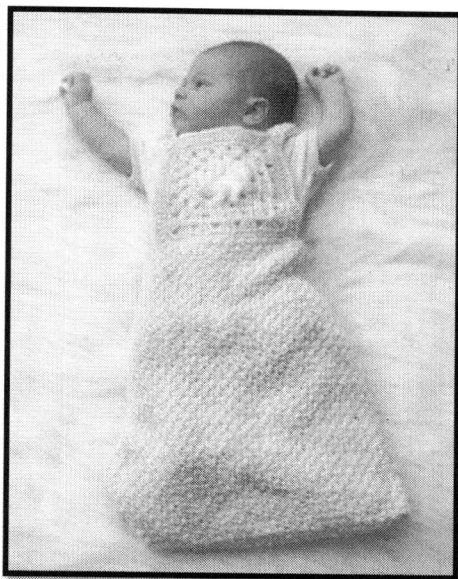

MATERIALS

1) Two Different Colors of Yarn – One Color with (Two Balls) and The Other Color with (One Ball)
2) Two Buttons
3) Size 3.75 mm (U.S. F or 5) Crochet Hook

MEASUREMENTS

Approximately Twenty-Four Inches [Sixty-One Centimeters] Around x Twenty-One Inches [Fifty-Three Point Five Centimeters} Long.

GAUGE

Seventeen Single Crochet and Twenty Rounds = Four Inches [Ten Centimeters].

INSTRUCTIONS

Notes:

Chain three at the beginning of the round counts as double crochet throughout the process.

When the joining colors, work to the last two loops on the hook of the first color. Pull the yarn of the new color through the last two loops and continue.

Front Motif

Using Color B, chain four. Join with a slip stitch to the first chain to form a ring.

First Round: Chain one. Work eight single crochet in the ring. Join with a slip stitch to the first single crochet.

Second Round: Chain three. Four double crochet in the first single crochet. Turn. Chain three. One double crochet in each of the next three double crochet. One double crochet in the top of chain three. Turn. * Chain four. Keeping chain four just worked behind the last petal made, five double crochet in the next single crochet. Turn. Chain three. One double crochet in each of the next three double crochet. One double crochet in the top of chain three. Turn. Repeat from * six times more. Chain four. Keeping chain four just working behind the last petal made, join with a slip stitch in top of the beginning of chain three.

Third Round: Join Color A with a slip stitch in any four space chain. Chain three. (Two double crochet. Chain two. Three double crochet) in the same four space chain. * Chain one. One single crochet in the next four space chain. Chain one. (Three double crochet. Chain two. Three double crochet) in the next four space chain. Repeat from * two more times. Chain one. One single crochet in the next four-space chain. Chain one. Join with a slip stitch to the top of chain three.

** Fourth Round: Slip stitch in each of the next two double crochet and next two-space chain. Chain three. (Two double crochet. Chain two. Three double crochet) in the same two space chain. * (Chain one. Three double crochet in the next one space chain) two times. Chain one. (Three double crochet. Chain two. Three double crochet) in the next two space chain. Repeat from * two more times. (Chain one. Three double crochet in the next one space chain) two times. Chain one. Join with a slip stitch to the top of chain three.

Fifth Round: Slip stitch in each of the next two double crochet and the next two-space chain. Chain three. (Two double crochet. Chain two. Three double crochet) in the same two space chain. * (Chain one. Three double crochet in the next one space chain) three more times. Chain one. (Three double crochet. Chain two. Three double crochet) in the next two space chain. Repeat from * two more times. (Chain one. Three double crochet in the next one space chain) three more times. Chain one. Join with a slip stitch to the top of chain three.

Sixth Round: Chain one. One single crochet in each double crochet or one space chain around, working three single crochet in each corner two space chain. Join with a slip stitch to the first single crochet. Fasten off.

Edging Round: Right Side. Join Color A with a slip stitch in any corner single crochet. Chain three. One double crochet in each of the next twenty-one stitches up side of Motif. (Two double crochet. Chain two. Two double crochet) in the corner single crochet. One double crochet in each of the next twenty-one stitches across the top of the Motif. (Two double crochet. Chain two. Two double crochet) in the corner single crochet. One double crochet in each of the next twenty-two stitches down side of the Motif. Fasten off (Bottom edge of the Motif is left unworked). **

Back Motif

Using Color A, chain four. Join with a slip stitch to the first chain to form a ring.

First Round: Chain three. Two double crochet in the ring. (Chain two. Three double crochet in the ring) three more times. Chain two. Join with a slip stitch to the top of chain three.

Second Round: Slip stitch in each of the next two double crochet and the next two-space chain. Repeat from * two more times. Chain one. Join with a slip stitch to the top of chain three.

Third Round: Slip stitch in each of the next two double crochet and the next two-space chain. Chain three. (Two double crochet. Chain two. Three double crochet) in the same two space chain. * Chain one. Three double crochet in the next one space chain. Chain one. (Three double crochet. Chain two. Three double crochet) in the next two space chain. Repeat from * two more times. Chain one. Three double crochet in the next one space chain. Chain one. Join with a slip stitch to the top of chain three. Repeat from ** to ** as given for Front Motif.

Body

First Round: Right Side. Join Color A with a slip stitch to the lower edge of the Back Motif. Chain one. Work twenty-five single crochet evenly across the lower edge of the Back Motif. Chain one. Work twenty-five single crochet evenly across the lower edge of the Motif. Chain twenty-eight. Work twenty-five single crochet evenly across the lower edge of the Front Motif. Chain twenty eight. Join with a slip stitch to the first single crochet.

Second Round: Chain one. One single crochet in the first single crochet. (One double crochet in the next single crochet. One single crochet in the next singe crochet) twelve more times. (One double crochet in the next chain. One single crochet in the next chain) fourteen more times. (One double crochet in the next single crochet. One single crochet in the next single crochet) twelve more times. One double crochet in the next single crochet. (One single crochet in the next chain. One double crochet in the next double crochet) fourteen times more. Join with a slip stitch to the first single crochet. One hundred and six stitches.

Third Round: Slip stitch in the next double crochet. Chain one. One single crochet in the same space. * One double crochet in the next single crochet. One single crochet in the next double crochet. Repeat from * around ending with one double crochet in the last single crochet. Join with a slip stitch to the first single crochet. Repeat the last round for the pattern until the Body measures fourteen inches [thirty-five point five centimeters]. Fasten off – Turn the work inside out. Fold the work and join the lower edge with one round of single crochet. Fasten off.

Straps (Make Two)

Using Color A, chain twenty six.

First Round: Right Side. One single crochet in the second chain from the hook. One single crochet in each chain to the end of the chain. Twenty-five single crochet. Turn.

Second Round: Chain two (does not counts as a half double crochet). One half double crochet in each stitch to the end of the round. Turn.

Third Round: Chain one. One single crochet in each half double crochet to the end of the round. Fasten off. Using a thread and needle, sew the ends of the Straps to the top edge of the Back Motif. Then attach one button on the opposite end of each Strap. Use the two-space chain in the edging at each corner of the Front Motif for buttonholes.

BABY PASTEL RIPPLY BLANKET

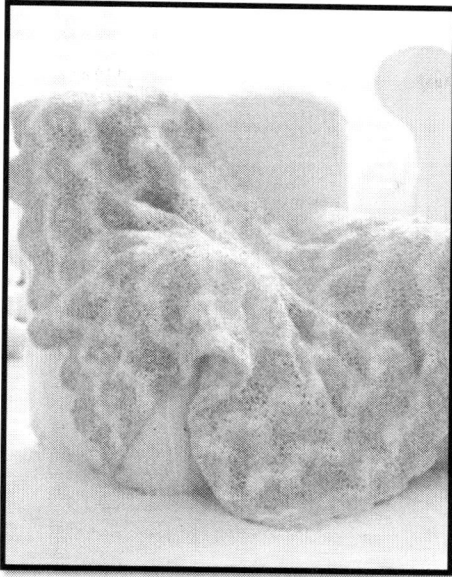

MATERIALS

1) Five Colors of Yarn – Two Balls Each
2) Size 5 mm (U.S. H/8) Crochet Hook

MEASUREMENTS

Approximately Thirty-Four Inches x Thirty Six and a Half [Eighty Six and a Half x Ninety-Two and a Half Centimeters].

GAUGE

Fifteen Single Crochet and Sixteen Rounds = Four Inches [Ten Centimeters].

INSTRUCTIONS

STRIPE PAT:

(Four Rounds of Color A. Two Rounds of Color B) two more times.
(Four Rounds of Color C. Two Rounds of Color B) two more times.

(Four Rounds of Color D. Two Rounds of Color B) two more times.
(Four Rounds of Color E. Two Rounds of Color B) two more times.

These forty eight rounds form Striped Pattern.

Using Color one hundred and fifty five chains.

First Round: Right Side. One double crochet in the fourth chain from the hook. (Double crochet to the next two stitches together over the next two chains) six more times. Chain one. (One double crochet in the next chain. Chain one) five more times. Repeat from * to the last six chains. (Double crochet the next two chains) three more times. Turn.

Second Round: Chain three. Miss the first stitch. One double crochet in the next stitch. (Double crochet the next two stitches together over the next stitch and the next one space chain) two more times. Chain one. One double crochet in the next double crochet. Chain one. (One double crochet in the next one space chain. Chain one. One double crochet in the next double crochet. Chain one) two more times. * (Double crochet the next two stitches together over the next one space chain and the next stitch) two more times. (Double crochet the next two stitches together over the next two stitches) two more times. (Double crochet the next two stitches together over the next stitch and the next one space chain) two more times. Chain one. One double crochet in the next double crochet. Chain one. (One double crochet in the next one space chain. Chain one. One double crochet in the next double crochet. Chain one) two more times. Repeat from * to the last two one space chains. (Double crochet the next two stitches together over the next one space chain and the next stitch) two more times. Double crochet the next two stitches together over the next two stitches. Turn. Leave turning the chain three unworked. First the two rounds of the Striped Pattern are complete. Keep continuing the Striped Pattern, repeat second round for pattern until forty eight rounds of Striped Pattern are finished.

Using Color A, work four rounds in pattern.
Using Color B, work four rounds in pattern.
Using Color A, work four rounds in pattern. Fasten off.

Side Edging:

With the Right Side facing, join the Color A with a slip stitch in the top corner. Chain one. Work the single crochet evenly down the side edge. Fasten off. Repeat on the opposite side edge.

BABY BLANKET

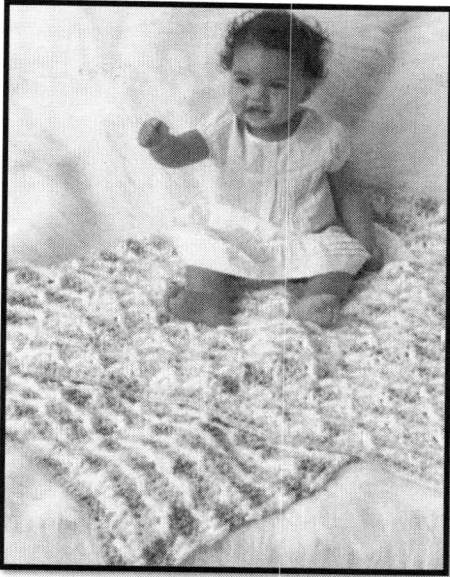

MATERIALS

1) Two Different Colored Yarn – Four Balls Each
2) Size 9 mm (U.S. M or 13) Crochet Hook

MEASUREMENT

Approximately Thirty-Four Inches [Eight Six and a Half Centimeters] Square.

GAUGE

Seven Double Crochet and Four Rounds = Four Inches [Ten Centimeters].

INSTRUCTIONS

Notes:

When joining different colors, work to the last two loops on the hook of the first color. Pull the new color through the last two loops and continue one. Chain three at the beginning fo the round counts as a double crochet throughout the process.

Stripe Pattern

Using the Main Color, work one round. Using Color A, work one round. These two rounds form a Stripe Pattern. Using the Main Color, chain sixty-four.

First Round: Wrong Side. One double crochet in the fourth chain from hook (counts as two double crochet). One double crochet in each chain to the end of the chain. Join Color A. Turn. Sixty-two double crochet.

Second Round: Using Color A, chain three. One double crochet in the next double crochet. * Miss the next two double crochet. One triple crochet in the next double crochet. Working behind the triple crochet just made, one double crochet in each of the missed two double crochet. Miss the next stitch (where the triple crochet is worked). One double crochet in each of the next two double crochet. Working in front of the double crochet just made, one triple crochet in the same space as the last triple crochet made. Repeat from * ten more times. Miss the next two double crochet. One triple crochet in the next double crochet. Working behind the triple crochet just made, one double crochet in each of the missed two double crochet. Miss the next stitch (where the triple crochet is worked). One double crochet in each of the next two double crochet. Join Main Color. Turn.

Third Round: Using the Main Color, chain three. One double crochet in each of the next three double crochet. (Yarn over hook and draw up a loop in the next stitch. Yarn over hook and draw through two loops on hook) two more times. Yarn over hook and pull through all the loops on the hook – double crochet the next two stitches together made (one double crochet in each of the next four double crochet. Double crochet the next two stitches together) ten more times. One double crochet in each of the next six stitches. Join Color A. Turn. Sixty-two stitches.

Fourth Round: Using Color A, chain three. One double crochet in the next double crochet. Miss the next double crochet. * One double crochet in each of the next two double crochet. Working in front of the double crochet just made, one triple crochet in missed double crochet. Miss the next two double crochet. One triple crochet in the next double crochet. Working behind the triple just made, one double crochet in each of the missed two double crochet. Miss the next stitch (where triple crochet is worked). Repeat from * ten more times. One double crochet in each of the next two double crochet. Working in front of the double crochet just made, one triple crochet in the missed double crochet. One double crochet in each of the last two double crochet. Join the Main Color. Turn.

Fifth Round: Using the Main Color, chain three. One double crochet in each of the next six stitches. Double crochet the next two stitches together. (One double crochet in each of the next four double crochet. Double crochet the next two stitches together) ten times. One double crochet in each of the next four double crochet. Join Color A. Turn.

Sixth Round: Repeat the Second Round. First, the six rounds of the Striped Pattern are finished. Repeat the third to sixth rounds of Texture Pattern. Keep continuing the Stripe Pattern, continue the Texture Pattern until the work from the beginning measures approximately thirty-four inches [eight six and a half centimeters], ending with a right side round. Fasten off.

BABY BATH MITT

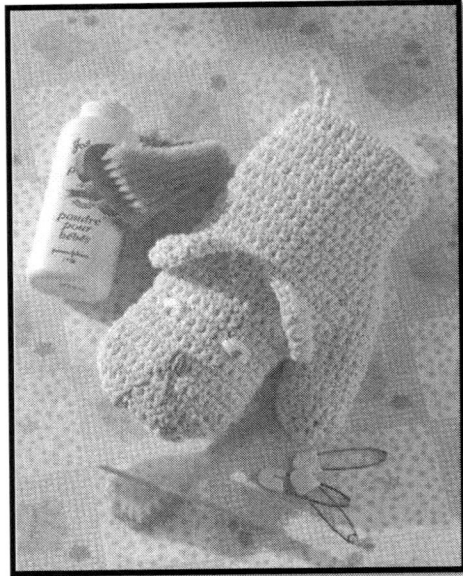

MATERIALS

1) One Color of Yarn – One Ball
2) Size 4.50 mm (U.S. 7) Crochet Hook
3) Small Amounts of White & Beige Yarn To Decorate and Embroider

SIZE:

To Fit an Adult.

GAUGE:

Fourteen Single Crochet and Sixteen Rounds = Four Inches [Ten Centimeters].

INSTRUCTIONS

Chain thirty-four.

First Round: Right Side. One single crochet in the second chain from the hook. One single crochet in each chain to the end of the chain. Thirty-three stitches. Chain one. Turn.

Second Round: One single crochet in each stitch to the end of the round. Chain one. Turn. Repeat the last round six more times.

Shape Thumb Gusset

First Round: Right Side. One single crochet in each of the first seventeen stitches. Two single crochet in each of the next two stitches. One single crochet in each of the stitch to the end of the round. Chain one. Turn.

Second and Every Even Number Until the Twelfth Round: One single crochet in eac stitch to the end of the round. Chain one. Turn.

Third Round: One single crochet in each of the seventeen stitches. Two single crochet in the next stitch. One single crochet in each of the next TWO stitches. Two single crochet in the next stitch. One single crochet in each stitch to the end of the round. Chain one. Turn.

Fifth Round: One single crochet in each of the seventeen stitches. Two single crochet in the next stitch. One single crochet in each of the next FOUR stitches. Two single crochet in the next stitch. One single crochet in each stitch to the end of the round. Chain one. Turn.

Seventh Round: One single crochet in each of the seventeen stitches. Two single crochet in the next stitch. One single crochet in each of the next SIX stitches. Two single crochet in the next stitch. One single crochet in each stitch to the end of the round. Chain one. Turn.

Ninth Round: One single crochet in each of the seventeen stitches. Two single crochet in the next stitch. One single crochet in each of the next EIGHT stitches. Two single crochet in the next stitch. One single crochet in each stitch to the end of the round. Chain one. Turn.

Eleventh Round: One single crochet in each of the seventeen stitches. Two single crochet in the next stitch. One single crochet in each of the next TEN stitches. Two single crochet in the next stitch. One single crochet in each stitch to the end of the round. Chain one. Turn.

Thirteenth Round: One single crochet in each of the first seventeen stitches. Chain two. Miss the next fourteen stitches. One single crochet in each of the stitch to the end of the round. Chain one. Turn.

Fourteenth Round: One single crochet in each stitch or one space chain to the end of the round. Thirty-three stitches. Continue even working until the work from the beginning measures eight inches [twenty and a half centimeters] ending with a Right Side facing for the next round.

Shape Top

First Round: One single crochet in the first stitch. Pull up a loop in each of the next two stitches. Yarn over hook and pull through all the three loops on hook – Single crochet the next two stitches together made. One single crochet in each of the next eleven stitches. Single crochet the next two stitches together. One single crochet in the next stitch. Single crochet the next two stitches together. One single crochet in each of the next eleven stitches. Single crochet the next two stitches together. One single crochet in the last stitch. Chain one. Turn.

Second Round: One single crochet in the first stitch. Single crochet the next two stitches together. One single crochet in each of the next NINE stitches. Single crochet the next two stitches together. One single crochet in the next stitch. Single crochet the next two stitches together. One single crochet in each of the next NINE stitches. Single crochet the next two stitches together. One single crochet in the last stitch. Chain one. Turn.

Third Round: One single crochet in the first stitch. Single crochet the next two stitches together. One single crochet in each of the next SEVEN stitches. Single crochet the next two stitches together. One single crochet in the next stitch. Single crochet the next two stitches together. One single crochet in each of the next SEVEN stitches. Single crochet the next two stitches together. One single crochet in the last stitch. Chain one. Turn.

Fourth Round: One single crochet in the first stitch. Single crochet the next two stitches together. One single crochet in each of the next FIVE stitches. Single crochet the next two stitches together. One single crochet in the next stitch. Single crochet the next two stitches together. One single crochet in each of the next FIVE stitches. Single crochet the next two stitches together. One single crochet in the last stitch. Chain one. Turn.

Fifth Round: One single crochet in the first stitch. Single crochet the next two stitches together. One single crochet in each of the next THREE stitches. Single crochet the next two stitches together. One single crochet in the next stitch. Single crochet the next two stitches together. One single crochet in each of the next THREE stitches. Single crochet the next two stitches together. One single crochet in the last stitch. Fasten off.

Thumb

With the Right Side of the work facing up, join the yarn with a single stitch to the chain space. Chain one. One single crochet in each of the next two chains. One single crochet in each of the next fourteen stitches. Join with a single stitch to the first single crochet. Sixteen single crochet.

Next Round: Chain one. One single crochet in each single crochet around. Join with a single stitch to the first single crochet. Repeat the last round four more times.

Next Round: Chain one. (Single crochet the next two stitches together) eight more times. Join with a single stitch to the first stitch. Eight stitches.

Next Round: Chain one. (Single crochet the next two stitches together) four more times. Four stitches. Fasten off. Thread the end through a tapestry needle and pull the yarn through the remaining stitches. Fasten securely.

Ear (Make Two)

Chain seven.

First Round: Right Side. One single crochet in the second chain from the hook. One single crochet in each of the next five chains. Chain one. Turn. Six stitches.

Second and Third Rounds: One single crochet in each stitch to the end of the round. Chain one. Turn.

Fourth Round: Single crochet the next two stitches together. One single crochet each of the next two stitches. Single crochet the next two stitches together. Chain one. Turn. Four stitches.

Fifth Round: (Single crochet the next two stitches together) two more times. Fasten off. Join the yarn with a single stitch to the side of the Ear at the lower corner and work one round of single crochet around the Ear to the opposite corner. Fasten off. Using a thread and needle, sew the Ears in position. Embroider the face. Now using a thread and needle, sew the top and the side seam.

Loop: Join the yarn with a single stitch at the lower side edge at the seam. Chain fifteen. Join with a single stitch in the same space as the first single stitch. Fasten off.

BABY SHAWL

MATERIALS

1) Six Balls of Yarn
2) Size 3.25 mm (U.S. D or 3) Crochet Hook

MEASUREMENTS:

Approximately Fifty-Three Inches [One Hundred and Thirty Four and a Half Centimeters] Wide and Thirty-Six Inches [Ninety-One and a Half Centimeters] Deep at the Centre.

GAUGE:

Three Shells and Thirteen Rounds = Four Inches [Ten Centimeters] in Pattern.

INSTRUCTIONS

Chain three hundred and sixteen.

First Round: One single crochet in the second chain from the hook. One single crochet in each chain to the end of the chain. Three hundred and fifteen single crochet. Chain one. Turn.

Second Round: Right Side. Miss the first single crochet. One single crochet in each of the next two single crochet. * Chain three. Miss the next two single crochet. (One double crochet. Chain three. One double crochet) in the next single crochet – V Stitch is made. Chain three. Miss the next two single crochet. One single crochet in each of the next three single crochet. Repeat from * to the end of the round. Chain four. Turn.

Third Round: * Seven double crochet in the three-space chain of the next V Stitch – Shell made. Chain three. Miss the next single crochet. One single crochet in the next single crochet. Chain three. Miss the next single crochet. Repeat form * ending the last repeat with one single crochet in the last single crochet. Chain six. Turn.

Fourth Round: * One single crochet in each of the next seven double crochet. Chain three. Repeat from * ending with one double crochet in the first chain of the turning chain. Chain six. Turn.

Fifth Round: * Miss the next two single crochet. One single crochet in each of the next three single crochet. Miss the next two single crochet. Miss the next chain. V Stitch in the next chain. Chain three. Miss the next chain. Repeat from * ending with miss the next two single crochet. One single crochet in each of the next three single crochet. Chain three. Miss the next two single crochet. One double crochet in the third chain of chain six. Turn.

Sixth Round: Single stitch in the first double crochet. Single stitch in teach of the next three chains. Single stitch in each of the next two single crochet. Chain four. * Seven double crochet in the three-chain space of the next V Stitch. Chain three. Miss the next single crochet. One single crochet in the next single crochet. Chain three. Miss the next single crochet. Repeat from * ending with seven double crochet in the three space chain of the last V Stitch. Chain three. Miss the next single crochet. One single crochet in the next single crochet. Chain six. Turn.

Seventh Round: * One single crochet in each of the next seven double crochet. Chain three. Repeat from * ending with one double crochet in the top of the last double crochet. Chain six. Turn.

Eighth Round: * Miss the next two single crochet. One single crochet in each of the next three single crochet. Miss the next two single crochet. Miss the next chain. V Stitch in the next chain. Chain three. Miss the next chain. Repeat from * ending with miss the next two single crochet. One single crochet in each of the next three single crochet. Chain three. Miss the next two single crochet. One double crochet in the third chain of chain six. Turn. Repeat the sixth to eighth rounds thirty six times more, then sixth round once omitting turning the chain at the end of the last round. (One shell remains). Fasten off.

Lower Edging

First Round: With the wrong side of the work facing upwards, join the yarn with a single stitch in the first chain of the starting chain. Chain one. One single crochet in the same space. One single crochet in each remaining loop of the starting chain. Three hundred and fifteen single crochet. Chain one. Turn.

Second and Third Round: Repeat the work that you have done for the main part of the blanket, however omitting the turning chain at the end of the third round. Fasten off.

BABY BIBS

MATERIALS

1) One Color of Yarn – One Ball
2) Size 5 mm (U.S. H or 8) Crochet Hook
3) Button

SIZE

To Fit the Baby: Newborn to Six Months.

GAUGE

13H Single Crochet and Sixteen Rounds = Four Inches [Ten Centimeters].

INSTRUCTIONS

BIB:

Chain twenty.

First Round: Right Side. One single crochet in the second chain from the hook. One single crochet in each chain to the end of the chain. Turn. Nineteen single crochet.

Second Round: Chain one. Two single crochet in the first stitch. One single crochet in each stitch to the last stitch. Two single crochet in the last stitch. Turn.

Third Round: Chain one. One single crochet in each stitch to the end of the round. Turn.

Fourth to Ninth Round: Two single crochet in the first stitch. One single crochet in each stitch to the last stitch. Two single crochet in the last stitch. Turn. One single crochet in each stitch to the end of the round. Turn. Two single crochet in the first stitch. One single crochet in each stitch to the last stitch. Two single crochet in the last stitch. Turn. One single crochet in each stitch to the end of the round. Turn. Two single crochet in the first stitch. One single crochet in each stitch to the last stitch. Two single crochet in the last stitch. Turn. One single crochet in each stitch to the end of the round. Turn. Twenty-seven single crochet. Continue doing this until the work from the beginning measures six inches [fifteen centimeters], ending with the right side facing up for the next round.

Shape Neck

First Round: Right Side. Chain one. One single crochet in each of the first six stitches. Pull up a loop in each of the next two stitches. Yarn over hook and pull through all three loops on the hook – single crochet the next two stitches together is made. Turn. Leave the remaining stitches unworked.

Second Round: Chain one. Single crochet the next two stitches together over the first two stitches. One single crochet in each stitch to the end of the round. Turn.

Third Round: Chain one. Single crochet the next two stitches together over the last two stitches. Turn. Five stitches. Work ten rounds even.

Next Round: Wrong Side. Chain one. Two single crochet in the first stitch. Pattern to the last two stitches. Single crochet the next two stitches together. Turn.

Next Round: Chain one. Single crochet the next two stitches together. One single crochet in each stitch to the last stitch. Two single crochet in the last stitch. Turn. Repeat the last two rounds two more times. Fasten off. With the right side of the work facing up, miss the next eleven stitches. Join the yarn with a slip stitch to the next stitch. Chain one. Single crochet the next two stitches together over this stitch and the next stitch. One single crochet in each stitch to the end of the round. Turn. Work to correspond to the first side, reversing all the different shapings.

Edging:

Join the yarn with a slip stitch to the top left one of the neck edge. Chain one. One single crochet in the same space as the last slip stitch. Work one round single crochet evenly around. Join with a slip stitch to the first single crochet.

Next Round: Working around the outer edge only, chain one. * One single crochet in each of the next three stitches. Chain three. Slip stitch in the first chain – picot made. Repeat from * to the top right hand corner. Chain six for the button loop. One single crochet in the next space. Fasten off. Using a thread and needle, sew the button in position.

BABY BOOTIES

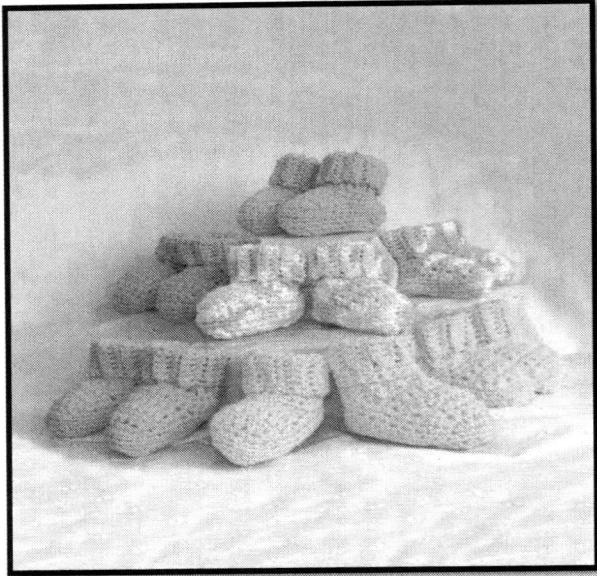

MATERIALS

1) One Color of Yarn – One Ball
2) Size 5 mm (U.S. H or 8) Crochet Hook
3) Button

SIZE

To Fit the Baby: Newborn to Six Months.

GAUGE

13H Single Crochet and Sixteen Rounds = Four Inches [Ten Centimeters].

INSTRUCTIONS

Chain fourteen.

First Round: Right Side. One single crochet in the second chain from hook. One single crochet in each chain to the end of the chain. Turn. Thirteen single crochet.

Second Round: Chain one. Working in the back loops only, one single crochet in each stitch to the end of round. Turn. Repeat the last round for 6G inches [16 centimeters] when slightly stretched. Do not fasten off.

First Round: Right Side. Chain one. Work twenty three single crochet evenly across the long edge of the cuff. Turn.

Second Round: Chain one. Work one single crochet in each single crochet to the end of the round. Fasten off.

Instep

First Round: With the right side of the work facing up, miss the first seven stitches, Join the yarn with a slip stitch to the next stitch. Chain one. One single crochet in the same space. One single crochet in each of the next eight stitches. Turn. Nine stitches.

Second to Fourth Rounds: Chain one. One single crochet in each stitch to the end of the round. Turn.

Fifth Round: Chain one. Single crochet the next two stitches together over the first two stitches. One single crochet in each of the next FIVE stitches. Single crochet the next two stitches together over the next two stitches. Turn.

Sixth Round: Chain one. Single crochet the next two stitches together over the first two stitches. One single crochet in each of the next THREE stitches. Single crochet the next two stitches together over the next two stitches. Fasten off. Using a thread and needle, sew the center back seam. With the right side of the work facing, join the yarn with a slip stitch at the center back. Chain one. One single crochet in each of the next seven stitches. Five single crochet down the side of the instep. Three single crochet in the corner single crochet. Three single crochet across the end of the instep. Three single crochet in the corner single crochet. Five single crochet along the other side of the instep. One single crochet in each of the next seven stitches. Join with a slip stitch to the first stitch. Thirty-three stitches.

Next Round: Chain one. One single crochet in each stitch around. Join with a slip stitch to the first stitch.

Next Round: Chain one. Working in the back loops only, work one single crochet in each stitch around. Join with a slip stitch to the first stitch.

Next Round: Chain one. Single crochet the next two stitches together. One single crochet in each of the next TWELVE stitches. Single crochet the next two stitches together. One single crochet in the next stitch.

Single crochet the next two stitches together. One single crochet in each of the next TWELVE stitches. Single crochet the next two stitches together. Join with a slip stitch to the first stitch.

Next Round: Chain one. Single crochet the next two stitches together. One single crochet in each of the next TEN stitches. Single crochet the next two stitches together. One single crochet in the next stitch. Single crochet the next two stitches together. One single crochet in each of the next TEN stitches. Single crochet the next two stitches together. Join with a slip stitch to the first stitch.

Next Round: Chain one. Single crochet the next two stitches together. One single crochet in each of the next EIGHT stitches. Single crochet the next two stitches together. One single crochet in the next stitch. Single crochet the next two stitches together. One single crochet in each of the next EIGHT stitches. Single crochet the next two stitches together. Join with a slip stitch to the first stitch. Fasten off. Using a thread and needle, sew the sole seam.

Printed in Great Britain
by Amazon